A Sticky Business

By Joy Cowley

Illustrated by Patricia Ludlow

Dominie Press, Inc.

Publisher: Christine Yuen
Editor: John S. F. Graham
Designer: Lois Stanfield
Illustrator: Patricia Ludlow

Published by:

⊕ Dominie Press, Inc.

1949 Kellogg Avenue
Carlsbad, California 92008 USA

www.dominie.com

Paperback ISBN 0-7685-1067-8
Library Bound Edition ISBN 0-7685-1482-7
Printed in Singapore by PH Productions Pte Ltd
  3 4 5 6 PH 04 03

Table of Contents

Chapter One

On the Sidewalk

At 4:30 in the afternoon,
outside the pet food shop,
Leroy Cardno sneezed.
His super-sticky bubble gum
shot out of his mouth
and landed on the sidewalk.

At the same time,
Mr. Mario, the lion-keeper,
was whistling a happy tune
while he walked to the store
to get pet food for his lions.

He stepped on the gum.

The walking stopped.
The whistling stopped.
Mr. Mario's shoe was stuck
to the sidewalk.

Chapter Two

Let Me Help You

"Oh, crabapple!"
cried Mr. Mario.
"I stepped on something sticky!"

"I'm sorry!" said Leroy Cardno.
"It's my fault. Let me help you."

Leroy grabbed Mr. Mario
by the ankle and pulled.
The shoe stayed stuck.

"Hurry!" cried Mr. Mario.

Leroy tried again. He said,
"You can take your foot
out of your shoe."

Mr. Mario shook his head.
"There's a hole in my shoe.
My foot's stuck, too."

"I'll get my mother,"
said Leroy Cardno.
"She's a doctor.
She'll know what to do."

Mr. Mario sighed.
"My lions are waiting
for their supper."

Chapter Three

The Lions Are Hungry

Mr. Mario's three lions
waited and waited
for their keeper.

They were hungry,
and they were worried.

Mr. Mario was never late.
What had happened to him?

At 5:30 in the afternoon,
one of the lions
put her paw through the bars
of the lion park gate.

She clicked the latch.
The gate swung open.

One by one, the lions
ran out of the park.
They went downtown
to look for Mr. Mario.

Chapter Four

This Is Not a Job
for a Doctor

Leroy Cardno's mother
looked at Mr. Mario's shoe.
"This is not a job
for a doctor," she said.

"I can't stay here forever!"
cried Mr. Mario.
"I have to feed my lions!"

"We'll call the police,"
said Leroy Cardno's mother.
"They'll know what to do."

"Oh, crabapple!"
sighed Mr. Mario.

Chapter Five

A Discussion about Bubble Gum

At 6:00 in the evening, three police officers came in a blue squad car.

They looked at Mr. Mario's shoe.
"This is not a job for the police,"
said one of the officers.
"We should call the fire department."

In a matter of minutes,
two red fire engines
with ten firefighters
rushed down the street.

"A stuck foot?" they cried.

"Bubble gum?" they cried.

"This is not a job
for the fire department.
Why did you call us?"

Then the firefighters,
the police officers,
and Leroy Cardno's mother
had a discussion
about super-sticky bubble gum
and who should help with it.

Mr. Mario cried, "My poor lions!
Oh my! Oh me! Oh crabapple!"

Chapter Six

Lions!

Soon after 6:30 in the evening,
the lions found Mr. Mario.
They bounded up the street,
roaring with happiness.

"Lions!" cried the firefighters,
running for their fire engines.

"Lions!" cried the police officers,
jumping into their squad car.

"Lions!" cried Leroy Cardno's mother,
dragging her son into the pet shop.

"My wonderful lions!"
cried Mr. Mario,
his arms held out wide.

The lions ran to their keeper
and licked his face.

"They're eating him!"
cried Leroy Cardno's mother.

"No, they're just tasting him,"
Leroy Cardno replied.

His mother grumbled. "I told you
that super-sticky bubble gum
would be big trouble."

Chapter Seven

Tired of Being Sticky

By 7:00 in the evening,
the fire engines
and squad cars had gone.
The shoe came unstuck.
No one knew how.
Maybe the lions did it.
Maybe the super-sticky bubble gum
got tired of being super-sticky.

Mr. Mario bought pet food
and gave his beautiful lions
an extra helping.

As for Leroy Cardno,
he went home
and put the rest
of his super-sticky bubble gum
in his mother's trash can.
The only trouble was,
no one could empty the trash.

It was stuck fast.